NATIONAL GEOGRAPHIC

The Earth

Trent Johnson

This is the Earth.

Some of the Earth is land.

Some of the Earth is water.

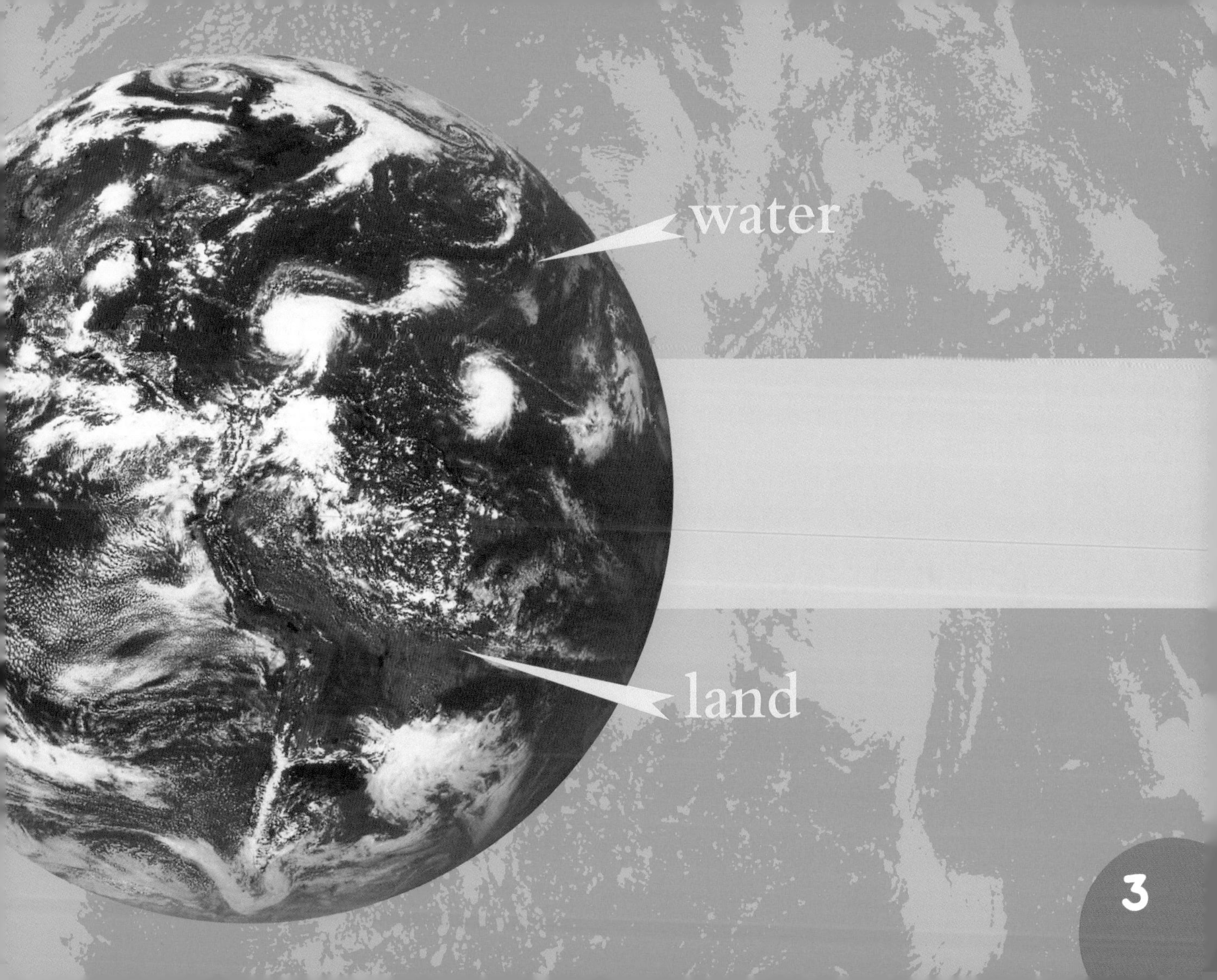
water
land

Some of the land is flat.
Land that is flat
is called a plain.

Some of the land is hilly.
Land that is hilly and high
is called a **mountain**.

7

Some of the land
is surrounded by water.
Land that is surrounded
by water is called an island.

Some of the water
is surrounded by land.
Water that is surrounded
by land is called a lake.

Some of the water flows
in big streams.
Water that flows
in big streams
is called a river.

This is the Earth.

The Earth has

plains

mountains

islands

lakes

rivers

Index